Purchased in Country kitchen
Gourmet in Jamestown, GA. 4/25/85
by M.G. Herbert

SHORT LINE TO PARADISE

"The Story of the Yosemite Valley Railroad"

SHORT LINE TO PARADISE

"The Story of the Yosemite Valley Railroad"

by HANK JOHNSTON

Published by Flying Spur Press
Box 278, Yosemite, California 95389
Copyright 1962, All Rights Reserved
Revised Second Edition, Copyright 1971

TRANS-ANGLO BOOKS

Fourth Edition (Revised) — 2nd Printing, June, 1975
Library of Congress Catalog No.: 70-166295
ISBN: 0-87046-022-6

Trade Distribution:
TRANS-ANGLO BOOKS
P.O. Box 38
Corona del Mar, Calif. 92625

LEFT: *Early YV motor car at El Portal. Man in derby is Frank L. Higgins,*
YV Motor Power Superintendent 1906-1941. (Clara Boyd Collection)

ACKNOWLEDGEMENTS

The compilation of material for this book would have been impossible without the gracious assistance of the following: Miss Marian Marvin of the Merced County Free Library; former YV employees L. A. Foster, William St. Jeor, Charles Wright and Melvin Williams; Mrs. Thora Adams, Mrs. Grace Christopherson, Mrs. Clara Boyd and Mrs. Dorthea Williams, all of Merced; Leon Bartholomew of Santa Barbara, J. M. McFadden of Palm Springs and Don Kracke of Long Beach.

To these persons and to all others whose names appear in the photo credits, the author is deeply indebted.

PRECEDING: *Last log train from Incline, Nov. 21, 1942 at Bagby. (Bob Lunoe)* RIGHT: *Henry Hedges who drove the first stagecoach into Yosemite Valley in July, 1874. (Title Insurance & Trust Co.)*

INTRODUCTION

There are those who say that the Yosemite Valley in the Springtime is the most beautiful spot on the face of the earth. "The only place I have ever found that came up to the brag" was Emerson's tribute long ago.

And who, indeed, can truly disparage the Cyclopean wonders of this paradise? Where else such breathtaking cascades of water hurtling thousands of feet in full flight? Where else such giants of granite, such titan rocks, such meadows of green framed by snow capped peaks on every side?

The very names quicken the heartbeat: El Capitan, Lost Arrow, Cloud's Rest, Bridalveil, Half Dome . . . the list is endless.

Down the middle of this magnitude like a fillet of steel flows the omnipresent Merced, a stream of many moods, changing in a turn from quiet water to roaring rapids, and bounding over the rocks like a many legged acrobat at play as it forces its relentless path to the sea.

Small wonder the sight-seers came a hundred years ago and have never ceased to come in ever-increasing numbers. A few came at first, on foot and by horseback. Then more, by wagon and stage as crude roads were built over the summits. And finally, they came by railroad and motor car in such hordes that the valley became a summer sea of humanity.

It is the railroad with which this book is concerned. It was called the Yosemite Valley Railroad, and its two score years of existence deserve a richer epitaph than can be given by a two-line listing in a tourist's guide book.

Here was a short line that had everything: a twisting, turning path of 70 lb. rail hugging the Merced most of the way through magnificent scenery; romantic lineside industries including gold mines and the steepest logging incline ever built; the grandest of passenger lists — Presidents, Kings, Hollywood celebrities, nabobs with their private cars, happy honeymooners on a once-in-a-lifetime trip, and plain garden-variety tourists out to see the sights on a one week vacation.

There was nothing but steam on the head end, and nothing but joy in the heart for 38 years.

Yes, the Yosemite Valley was truly a short line that had everything, and one thing more . . . it was a

SHORT LINE TO PARADISE

THIS IS HER STORY

The Yosemite Valley Railroad was conceived when the century, like the land, was young and filled with the hope and promise of an expanding America.

It was thought at the time to be the ultimate answer to the need for an easier, faster route to Yosemite National Park and its builders confidently predicted it would last for 200 years. Their optimism in financing a railroad through the California wilderness between Merced and the valley was based on the tremendous tourist appeal that the

LEFT: *Camp Curry in 1902. Signs show rates at $2 per day and also advertise the Coulterville Stage as the cheapest way out of the valley.* RIGHT: *Inspection trip to Yosemite Valley in 1906. Man on left is Charles Wright, YV traffic agent, and his companion is Frank Higgins, motive power boss. The two officials had traveled to the valley from end of track during construction.*

Yosemite had exerted since it was first visited by sight-seers in 1855.

The early travelers endured unbelievable hardships to view the wonders. One hardy pioneer, who was advised to move rapidly along an Indian trail or lose his scalp, replied, "If my hair is now required, I can deposit in peace for I have seen the power and the glory of the Supreme Being."

Access to the valley improved when the Central Pacific extended its lines to Merced about the time the first stage roads were opened in the 1870's, but the overland trip still required two days of hard going each way. Surveys were made for a railroad as early as 1890 and rumors of impending construction were widely circulated, but un-expected opposition was encountered from "nature cranks" as they were dubbed by advocates of easier transportation. These critics maintained that the beauties of the Yosemite should not be cheapened and brought within the compass of the troubled many, while the supporters of the other idea wanted equal rights of scenery as well as constitution and proclaimed that there was no reason that a man in a clean shirt could not appreciate nature as deeply as a chap with his lungs full of dust, a crimp in his collar and an ache in his back.

The general feeling at the time was that it would be either the Southern Pacific or the Santa Fe who would eventually build a line into the valley, but neither of these giants deemed the idea a practical one. Instead, it was a group of Oakland and San Francisco financiers who took the initiative by incorporating the Yosemite Valley Railroad Company on December 18, 1902, under the general laws of the State of California for a period of 50 years. Principal officers were Frank G. Drum, president, Thomas Prather, vice-president and William W. Garthwaite, secretary-treasurer.

Acquisition of right-of-ways into the valley delayed construction for nearly three years, but finally, working through Congress, YV officials managed to obtain a path through forest reserves to the very edge of the park itself.

In September, 1905, construction crews began the difficult task of grading, surfacing and track laying. From Merced, the western terminus, the first 24 miles were laid swiftly as the route headed in a nearly straight line across the level San Joaquin Valley. From Merced Falls on, the railroad was constructed through the canyon of the Merced River in rough foothill and mountainous country. Wagon roads and trails had to be built to connect with existing highways. In transporting supplies and equipment only

YOSEMITE VALLEY RR

Legend

1 — Merced	11 — Bagby
2 — Merced River Bridge	12 — Kocher
3 — Snelling	13 — Saxon Creek
4 — Merced Falls	14 — Briceburg
5 — Entrance to Merced Canyon	15 — Woody
6 — Exchequer Dam	16 — Clearinghouse
7 — Barrett Bridge	17 — Incline
8 — Jasper	18 — El Portal, end of line
9 — Detwiler	19 — Floor of Yosemite Valley
10 — Kittredge	20 — Glacier Point
	21 — Mariposa Grove of Big Trees

N

Contractor James O'Brien hired construction workers from surrounding areas with some coming from as far as San Francisco. Ad from a 1906 Merced newspaper is shown above. Local farmers complained about lack of extra harvest workers during the building of the YV because of higher railroad wages.

FREIGHT AND TICKET OFFICE

pack horses could be used in reaching some of the work and considerable material was lowered to camp sites by ropes and sleds from the rim of the canyon. A steam shovel was used at only one location and for most excavation, two-wheeled horse carts, wheelbarrows and drags were extensively employed.

Construction was done principally by company forces under James H. O'Brien, San Francisco contractor, and N. C. Ray, a Coulterville mining superintendent who served as chief engineer from 1903 until 1906. Ray acquired much of the right of way on various Washington trips and did the bulk of the early surveying. He was replaced in 1906 by Grant H. Nickerson who supervised the route from Detwiler on and remained as YV chief engineer until retirement in 1928.

Stories of the progress appeared in San Francisco newspapers with such items listed as 2,800,999 lbs. of black powder and dynamite for blasting, and a cost of $65 in wages to transport a light pushcart less than a mile. Another report tells of it taking a "great horde of men more than 10 months to hew 2 miles of roadway through a precipitous box canyon."

Certainly it was difficult going for the hard-drinking, two-fisted group of 1500 workers that blasted through the sandstone and granite walls all the way to the very gates of the National Park, but some of the exploits may have been slightly enlarged.

The roadway had a maximum grade of 1% for the first 70 miles, then 2% for 2 miles, and the rest of the grade varied between 1% and 2% in a total rise of 1900 feet on the entire route.

Grades were encountered on 63.5 miles of line and for 32.9 miles the line was on curves. Maximum curvature was 15 degrees except at Hog Back where there was one 18 degree curve. The track crossed the Merced River three times and once laid, the original line was never changed except for the Exchequer Dam relocation in 1926.

13

LEFT: *El Portal area in June, 1907. Note construction activity with Hotel Del Portal in background and temporary station at left front.* (*Oakland Tribune*) RIGHT: *Typical right-of-way through Merced Canyon near Milepost 63.* (*Fred Stoes*)

The main line Bessemer rail weighed 70 lbs. to the yard and other tracks were laid with both 70 lb. and 45 lb. new rail and 65 lb. relay rail, all to standard gauge. There were 505 curves on the 78.43 miles of route plus 10.265 miles of yards and sidings.

On April 26, 1906, the first locomotive ran the 24 miles to Merced Falls and shortly after, regular service began on the Merced-Snelling-Merced Falls portion to connect with the Yosemite Transportation Stage for Coulterville, Mariposa and Yosemite Valley. In June, 1906, the Native Sons of the Golden West, Merced Parlor, held a picnic in Snelling, original seat of Merced County. The YV carried 1,100 persons from Merced to join the celebration. It was reported as "the grandest affair of its kind in the history of Merced County."

By May, 1907, the rails had reached El Portal (the gate) which became the end of track, partly because of the steep grades from this point on, and partly because of the difficulty in obtaining further right-of-way from the Park Service. An 8 mile wagon road was built into the valley instead, at a cost to the railroad of $73,260.24.

On May 15, 1907, the first full length run of the YVRR left Merced bound for El Portal carrying 12 passengers. There was little fanfare and no demonstration, but the railroad was at last in business although considerable work yet remained on the line.

Once the YV was a reality, various stories appeared of competing lines and mergers. A San Francisco newspaper published a report of the sale of the YV to George Gould, head of the Western Pacific. Another paper stated that H. E. Huntington would have a great electric line into the valley from Fresno by 1908. Neither of these events ever took place, but it was obvious that the big railroads were jealous of the little YV as they refused to cooperate with ticket transfers and interchange freight for several years.

Various totals ranging up to $10,000,000 have been quoted as the cost of building the YV. The actual figure is difficult to determine accurately as many early company records were destroyed in the San Francisco fire of 1906. Probably the most correct tabulation is the value placed by the I.C.C. at a rate-making hearing required by the 1916 valuation law. After a lengthy discussion, the I.C.C. established a total cost of $3,356,492.00 for all property,

RIGHT: *No. 22 waits at El Portal with metal baggage-postal car 107 and wooden observation 330 in 1941. Trains were turned on a "Y" and backed into terminal during later years as early "armstrong" turntable operation proved unsatisfactory. (Larry Grabert)*

right-of-way and construction despite the YV's claim that the original cost was $4,274,603.74. The I.C.C. noted in its report that "many of the carrier's figures were not supported by proper documents and vouchers and a number of discrepancies in the carrier's claims were to be noted."

The YV had listed such items as: grading, $1,678,173.14; cost of lands, $12,276.74; bridges and culverts, $311,626.97; ties, $184,412.69 (mostly pine later replaced by longer-lasting redwood); rails, $438,959.32; and tracklaying and surfacing, $286,870.03, all of which the I.C.C. downgraded in valuation in varying degrees.

The financing of the railroad was accomplished by the establishment of a funded debt of $5,000,000 of which $3,000,000 represented first-mortgage 5% sinking-fund 30-year gold bonds due January 1, 1936, and $2,000,000 represented second-mortgage 5% sinking-fund 30-year gold bonds due January 1, 1936. The bonds were issued in $1000 amounts and were pursuant to a first mortgage to the Mercantile Trust Company of San Francisco, of which YV President Frank Drum was also an official. The corporation issued YV capital stock totaling $4,900,000 to Drum and his associates for "services rendered aggregating many thousands of dollars" but the actual amount of cash invested by the corporate officers was never determined

and undoubtedly the stock represented a well-watered figure.

In the long run, it was the inability of the railroad to ever satisfy the $3,000,000 first mortgage that eventually put it out of business 40 years later, but in 1907 all was optimism, trains were running on schedule, and the YV was expectantly awaiting the rush of tourists that would make it a profitable and going concern.

The listed address of the corporation was Drum's San Francisco office, but the actual operation of the line was carried on from the new Merced depot with Oliver W. Lehmer, former traffic manager for the Santa Fe at Stockton, as the first superintendent. Charles H. Wright, Lehmer's assistant at Stockton, was traffic agent and Grant Nickerson the chief engineer.

Early equipment consisted of four oil-burning American type locomotives, numbers 20, 21, 22 and 23, and a small group of cars including coach number 302 and observation number 330. In 1909, the YV leased three coaches from the Pullman Company agreeing to pay 2c per car, per mile, plus repairs and damages. The lease was signed by Robert Lincoln, the famous President's son and head of the Pullman Company at that time.

Exact dates of the procurement of other cars and equipment are uncertain but the I.C.C. valuation report of June 30, 1916, showed the YV with 6 steam locomotives, 193 freight cars, 5 passenger cars, 4 work cars and a Pierce-Arrow rail auto.

LEFT: *Merced depot shortly after completion in 1907.* (*Frank Robinson*) ABOVE: *Observation 330 at El Portal shed in 1938. This car was in operation during entire life of the YV.* (*Walt Masters*) RIGHT: *YV Motor Car No. 1 at Merced in the '20s. Note unusual rubber-tired, flanged wheels that were adopted after several broken axles resulted from use of regular rail wheels.* (*Clara Boyd collection*)

18

Perhaps the most historic piece of early motive power was engine number 21, obtained from the Wabash Railroad in 1906 along with engineer Charlie Grant. Grant hadn't intended to go to work for the YV at all as his original task was merely to deliver the engine to Merced for the Wabash. However he liked the new line so well that he stayed on to run old 21 until 1926 when he was retired with great ceremony. During his forty years of service on the Wabash and YV, Grant and his favorite engine never had an accident of any kind, not even a derailment.

LEFT: *Engine No. 21 at Merced yard after "retirement." (Fred Stoes)*
ABOVE: *Charlie Grant and son Jessie Grant, also a YV employee, at Merced in 1911 (Wahneta Hall collection)*
ABOVE RIGHT: *Resplendent No. 21 shortly after 1924 overhaul. Lettering "C. H. Grant" can be seen on cab.*

When number 21, which had been built in 1881, was overhauled in November, 1924, it was relettered "C. H. Grant" and the fading letters could still be seen on the side of the cab when the venerable engine was scrapped in 1946.

The battle for the tourist trade between the newly formed rail line and the horse-drawn stages was short lived with the YV an easy victor. In 1907, D. K. Stoddard, pioneer stage operator in Merced, moved his line to El

Portal where he carried passengers into the valley under a five-year contract. The railroad bought the stage line in 1911 and began using automobiles on a limited basis in 1912. Biggest day in the history of the horse-drawn stages was on June 6, 1909, when 68 stages pulled by 272 horses, carried 601 passengers from El Portal into the valley for a Knights of Columbus convention. All saloons were closed for the day so the drivers would remain sober.

From the beginning, the YV showed a steady increase in both passenger and freight revenue for 20 years. In 1907, passenger receipts totaled $61,105. This increased to $91,597 in 1908, $111,384 in 1909, and $151,792 in 1910. In 1912 a lumber mill was established by Milwaukee capital at Merced Falls and a spectacular incline was built at El Portal by YV chief engineer Nickerson for the new industry, the Yosemite Lumber Company. About 25 miles

of logging track ran from the top of the incline back to Empire Meadow and thousands of logs were lowered down the incline tracks to the waiting YV trains until the supply of timber dwindled in 1922. The crest of the incline was 3100 feet above the Merced and a right-of-way dropped for 8300 feet down the mountainside and across the river with a maximum grade in one spot of 78%.

The incline was moved in 1923 by a force of 200 men and a cost of $500,000, and set up across the river on the YV side of the Merced. New tracks were laid back into the woods from the top of the 8400 foot incline and Yosemite Lumber Company shays continued to haul their loads to the waiting gravity drop and the YV main line. The lumber company employed 500 men at the mill and another 500 in the woods during this period and had a summer payroll of $5500 a day. In 1924, the YV hauled 9204 carloads of logs to the mill at Merced Falls and 2253 carloads of lumber and box shooks from the mill to outgoing connections. A yearly cut of 75,000,000 board feet of lumber was not unusual at this time for the operation.

LEFT: *Yosemite Stage depot at Merced in 1904 with Santa Fe station in left background. Man second from right is D. K. Stoddard, owner of the stage line, and man fourth from right is Jim Leonard, early day stage driver who became the only person to work for the YV during its entire existence (1906-1946). (Grace Christopherson collection)* RIGHT: *First incline across from El Portal shortly after completion. Operations began on August 2, 1912, after more than a year of construction. (Dorthea Williams collection)*

Another important lineside industry was added to the railroad when the Yosemite Portland Cement Company was incorporated in 1925 for $1,500,000 by A. Emory Wishon of Fresno. YV cars were employed to haul limerock from the quarry at Emory to the mill at Merced, a distance of 67 miles. A half-mile incline was built from the Emory sidings up the side of an abrupt grade from where an internal combustion engine hauled the limerock from the quarry, another mile away.

A barytes mine at El Portal, mail and freight for the National Park, and a number of smaller mines and quarries all helped to swell the YV revenue until in 1925, total income was $1,409,986, largest in history, resulting in a net profit of $198,227 after paying fixed charges of $470,-986. Passenger travel reached its all-time high this same year with 85,107 persons paying $358,234 to ride the railroad.

But despite the ever-increasing income, net profits after fixed charges were reported only in 1907, 1916, 1923, 1925 and 1926. The fixed charges were the payment of the 5% interest on the $3,000,000 first mortgage and the required sinking-fund payments to retire the first-mortgage bonds. At no time during the life of the railroad was any interest or principal payment ever made on the $2,000,000 second mortgage, nor was any stock dividend ever paid.

Two major events occurred in the period between 1923 and 1926 that had a drastic effect on the YV operation. One was the building of the Exchequer Dam by the Merced Irrigation District, and the second, and most important, was the completion of the final leg of the all-year highway between Merced and the National Park.

The Exchequer Dam was built to harness the waters of the Merced River and relocate it in the canals of the irrigation system. It was financed by a bond issue and brought water to 125,000 acres of farmland, but it necessitated the relocation of 17 miles of YV main line. The cost of the relocation alone was $5,000,000 out of a total project expense of $15,000,000 and was paid by the Irrigation District. It consisted of the excavation of 1,500,000 cubic yards of earth, the building of 5 steel bridges and 2 trestles, the laying of 2165 gross tons of 70 lb. rail and the construction of 4 tunnels through solid rock for a total length of 3615 feet. A force of 666 men worked continuously on the project for nearly two years while the railroad continued to maintain its 22 trip daily schedule on the original line as it provided an access route for the

LEFT: *Contractor's engine and YV employees at Exchequer construction in 1923. Left to right — William Shay, Hubert McHugh, William Cobb and Melvin Williams.* ABOVE: *Partially completed Barrett span in 1924 clearly showing height of concrete pillars. (Both photos Melvin Williams collection)* BELOW: *View looking across bridge at high water. (Leon Bartholomew)*

contractor's engines and equipment. Several locomotives were borrowed from the Southern Pacific to haul cement and gravel to the construction site.

The dam itself was the largest project of its kind in America at that time. It was 330 feet high, 960 feet long, 16 feet in width at the top and 220 feet thick at the base. It required 396,000 cubic yards of concrete and provided a reservoir area of 2720 acres with a total capacity of 289,000 acre feet of water in its 12 mile length.

LEFT: *Yosemite Lumber Company log cars crossing the Barrett bridge on their way to the mill at Merced Falls.*
ABOVE: *First auto stage into Yosemite Valley from El Portal.*

Largest of the 5 steel bridges built for the railroad was the 1599.7 foot Barrett bridge, named for a pioneer rancher of the area. The base of the rail on the bridge was 236 feet above low water mark and nearly 5,000,000 lbs. of steel were used in the structure.

The first run over the newly relocated line was on April 18, 1926. When the new route was proclaimed satisfactory, Bent Brothers Contractors of Los Angeles who had built the dam, rushed every available man to work pouring concrete into the hole at the base of the dam through which YV trains had passed on the old run during construction. It took 7 days for the concrete to set before the waters could be run into the storage area and the former line

ABOVE: *Mixed train crossing Barrett Bridge Sept.* 4, 1944.

was then inundated to an average depth of 106 feet.

An unfavorable construction project was also being completed in 1926 when convict labor finished the last section of the all-year highway from Briceburg into Yosemite National Park. It was this road that hurt the YV more than anything else in its history. The Yosemite Transportation Co. immediately began offering trips originating at Merced rather than El Portal at lower rates than the railroad fare. Passenger revenue dipped 38% during the next year and decreased steadily from then on. The YV was defeated by the bus and auto competition almost as easily as the railroad itself had whipped the stages 20 years earlier.

Another blow fell on November 26, 1927 when the Yosemite Lumber Company closed its mill because of a decreasing market. The lumber company had been providing a major portion of YV freight revenue since its inception. In December, 1928, the Sugar Pine Lumber Company of Pinedale purchased the assets of Yosemite Lumber for $6,000,000 and reopened operations for a brief time but the depression hit in force in 1930 and the mill at Merced Falls closed completely for a 5 year period.

The YV attempted to fight the competition from the bus line by reducing fares from $13.50 in 1925 to $10.50 in 1929. It added a dining car and newer observation and inaugurated through sleeping car service from San Francisco and Los Angeles via the SP but even then only 25,912 passengers were carried in 1929. The railroad complained bitterly to the I.C.C. on several occasions that the bus rates from El Portal to the valley were much higher than from Merced to El Portal and asked the commission to fix the fares but to little avail. To add to the troubles, the main offices and depot at Merced were partly destroyed by fire in August, 1929, but were immediately rebuilt.

It was obvious that the YV was in serious trouble when it failed to make the required sinking-fund payment on the first mortgage for the first time in 1929, after reducing the $3,000,000 obligation by $682,000 at that date. The railroad failed to make the 5% interest payment on January 1, 1932 and a bond-holders committee was organized on October 25, 1932 to decide the future course of action.

The Portland Cement Company added to the YV woes by dropping its production 50% about this time and as a result of the lumber, cement and tourist drop offs, the

No. 28 switching at Merced in 1942. (Bob Lunoe)

railroad lost $62,956 in 1932 *before* fixed charges, the largest loss in its history.

In October, 1934, a group of bond holders representing the majority of first-mortgage bond holders incorporated the Yosemite Valley *Railway* Company and in effect took over the Yosemite Valley *Railroad* Company as bankruptcy receivers on December 23, 1935. The holders of the $2,000,000 second mortgage were eliminated by this action but the balance due on the first mortgage of $2,318,000 was still ominously present.

The road was put in the hands of a group of five trustee-directors representing the first-bond holders with Howard Bonsall, Los Angeles attorney, as chairman and president of the railroad. This management setup continued essentially unchanged for the remaining life of the YV although several reorganization plans were submitted and tentatively approved by the I.C.C. between 1937 and 1943.

After the 1935 reorganization, things improved somewhat for the next five years. The Sugar Pine Lumber Company obtained an RFC loan of $688,000 in 1935 and resumed its Merced Falls operation. Mail and tourist revenue improved each year and in 1939, a profit of $101,726 was realized before fixed charges.

Bagby Bridge after December, 1937, washout. Twisted rails at end of bridge demonstrate severity of damage. (William St. Jeor)

But one thing after another seemed to pop up unexpectedly to plague the YV whenever the situation seemed promising. On December 11, 1937, a disastrous flood of the Merced River washed out 30 miles of track in 'the canyon including the Bagby bridge. Traffic was suspended until May 16, 1938 when the first load of products from the Portland Cement plant at Emory made the Merced run. The cost of rebuilding the line damaged by the flood was $100,000, of which $75,000 was raised through a gift of $50,000 from the industries served and $25,000 from a rehabilitation loan from the SP and Santa Fe.

To compound the problems, combination 105 and observation 331, the YV's newest passenger cars were badly damaged by fire in October, 1937, and subsequently scrapped.

The Sugar Pine Lumber Company sold its major holdings to the government in 1940 and began closing out its operation. The last train of logs rolled down to Merced Falls on November 11, 1942, and the mill was shut down for the final time shortly after.

Adding more misery to the YV was the sale and disbandment of the Portland Cement Company quarry and plant in June, 1944. The company, which had been losing money for some time, sold out to Kaiser, its principal

Open White stage departing El Portal for Yosemite Valley in the 1920's. (NPS Photo)

competitor, for $565,000. The stockholders, who seemed quite happy to realize something on their investment, used the shaky position of the YV as an excuse for selling, but the truth seemed to be that the reasonable offer from Kaiser who wanted to eliminate the competition was too good to deny. Kaiser moved the machinery to Columbia, South America, and the railroad had lost a 25 car-a-day customer.

Passenger traffic dropped to 584 persons paying a total of $1958 in 1944 and freight revenue fell to $152,123. Net profit before fixed charges was $6486, however, due mainly to a reduction in personnel to 44 and a locomotive rental income from the SP of $31,578. But when the omnipresent bond interest of $116,349 was deducted, the net result was a tremendous deficit, as usual. The personnel total of 44 during this year can be compared to the peak times of the 1920's when 200 persons were employed with a payroll of $25,000 a month.

Regular mail service over the line was cancelled by the Navy in 1943 because of dissatisfaction with the irregular delivery and represented an income loss of $1600-$1800 a month. Daily train service was reduced to three trains a week in 1944 and finally, on August 31, the YV trustees applied to the I.C.C. for abandonment.

I.C.C. hearings began in Merced on December 1, 1944. About the only vociferous dissenter to abandonment was the National Lead Company whose baroid plant at El Portal now represented the bulk of YV freight traffic. Trustee

Bonsall in a lengthy testimony, described the various abortive reorganization attempts and W. L. White, long-time YV general manager, and L. A. Foster, then general manager, also presented evidence supporting abandonment. Both the National Park Service and the Yosemite Park and Curry Company took positions of neutrality. Finally, despite the appeals from National Lead, Robert Romero, I.C.C. examiner, ruled for abandonment on February 28, 1945, and the YV appeared doomed.

Two events occurred at this time, however, to liven up the interment proceedings considerably. One was an offer on January 8, 1945, by the Machine Tool and Equipment Company of New York to buy the 2318 outstanding $1000 first-mortgage bonds for $280 cash each, subject to 70% of the bond holders acceding. When the offer expired on March 23, 1945, 80% of the bonds had been exchanged, with the total reaching 96% shortly after. Thus the Machine Tool and Equipment Company, in effect, took over the ownership of the railroad and its assets and announced its intention to scrap the line.

In May, 1945, John M. McFadden, an 18 year-old junior engineer for the Pacific Electric Company from Pasadena, appeared on the scene and announced that he represented the Pacific Coast Railroading Association and

Engine and roundhouse crewmen posed on turntable with No. 26 at Merced in 1939.
Man in hat standing at left is W. L. White, longtime YV general manager. (Al Sheldon collection)

would like to buy the YV and continue its operation. Although it was uncertain as to how he intended to finance the purchase, McFadden received national publicity and a great deal of local support. President Adolph Freideberg of Machine Tool came to Merced and held several meetings with McFadden so the boy's offer of a reported $300,000 was apparently taken seriously by those concerned. Freideberg wanted $450,000 for the line, according to reports at the time, which McFadden refused to consider. Since McFadden's employer was the Pacific Electric, a subsidiary of the Southern Pacific. it was rumored that he actually represented the SP which received the bulk of interchange freight from the YV, but this allegation was denied by both McFadden and the railroad.

In the end, there was nothing but talk and the American Trust Company (successors to the Mercantile Trust Company) announced that the YV would be sold at public auction in San Francisco on September 7, 1945.

While all the legal machinations were taking place in the final few months of operation. one other catastrophe remained for the YV. On February 2, 1945, a flood second only to the 1937 deluge, engulfed a portion of the roadbed near Bagby. Torrential rains unloosened great landslides which covered the tracks and washed out nine supports

John M. McFadden, 18 year-old railfan, as he looked in 1945.

of the Bagby bridge. The YV was closed down for the second time in its history with thousands of dollars worth of damage to repair.

Engineer Bill Stipp, who was doubling as fireman for engineer Jack Shoup on the Kittridge-Bagby run on the day of the flood, told about the washout the next day: "The water was rising fast and lapping at the ties as we approached Bagby. I looked up and saw something coming toward us. I yelled at Shoup and told him a part of the Bagby bridge was floating toward us, and it was. Parts of the structure were adrift and the water had reached the top of the bridge piers. Shoup stopped and we backed up quickly to safety."

The line was back in service by February 16 after hurried repairs, and continued operation while abandonment proceedings were closing in. On August 20, just 4 days before the scheduled last run, a fire erupted in a pile of driftwood under the bedeviled Bagby bridge and 100 feet of the structure burned to the ground. The fire was believed to have been started by a cigarette carelessly tossed from a passing train. Engine number 28 and about $150,000 worth of equipment were marooned on the El Portal side of the burned-out bridge. There was some discussion about leaving the equipment for salvage,

No. 21 pulling 3 car passenger train through Box Canyon in June, 1907. Print from the original glass plate courtesy Oakland Tribune.

but in the end the bridge was patched up and all the remaining cars hauled back across.

The last run left Merced at 3:17 p.m., August 24, 1945, with engine number 23 pulling caboose number 19. The engineer was Jack Shoup with Robert Jirsa and Henry Loggins as brakemen on the abbreviated trip to Merced

Falls and return. With two carloads of zinc, bound eventually for Montana, the little train puffed into Merced for the last time at 5:18 p.m. Shoup tried to put on a good show for the handful of photographers and poured out so much smoke at one point that he started a local brush fire. It was a final brave gesture by the "Baby Road of the Mountains," as San Francisco papers had called it forty years earlier, but it died as it had begun with little fuss or fanfair.

Another figure arrived in the area about this time in the person of Al Perlman, chief engineer of the Denver and Rio Grande, who apparently came to lend his friend Mr. Friedeberg a helping hand in the proceedings although with no official interest that could be immediately determined. Mr. Perlman, in fact, represented the Machine Tool and Equipment Company in San Francisco when the auction took place at 10 a.m. on September 7, 1945, at the Polk Street entrance to the City Hall. Only others in attendance were McFadden's attorney and an observer for the Merced Chamber of Commerce. Neither one offered any competition to Perlman's bid of $585,000.

The winning offer was accompanied by a check for $27,270 which Perlman put up as payment to the approximate 4% of the remaining bond holders who had not

Last train leaving Merced Yard, 3:17 p.m., August 24, 1945.

Engineer Charlie Grant and crew with Engine No. 22 at Merced turntable in 1910. (Wahneta Hall Collection)

previously exchanged their bonds, and the balance of the $585,000 was more than covered by the 96% bondholding already acquired. The actual cost to Machine Tool to obtain the YV apparently was $280 times 2318 (the number of $1000 bonds outstanding) or a total of $649,040. What Al Perlman's interest in the proceeding was has never been explained, but one good guess would be that the D & RG needed scrap rail badly during the wartime shortage and it is significant to note that no rail ever appeared in the YV liquidation ads put out by Machine Tool and Equipment.

Whether the whole deal was a good financial investment for Mr. Friedeberg and his associates was never made public but there was a considerable drop in scrap prices between the time of the offer to buy the bonds and the actual sale of the railroad equipment, so the results may have been less than anticipated in any case. The YV had an estimated $450,000 in liquid assets, plus possibly $300,000 in scrap salvage, but the various attorney, bank and trustee charges plus the cost of dismantling the road and building a highway for the National Lead Company (as required by the I.C.C. as a condition of abandonment) may have nearly equaled the amount remaining after deducting the cost of the bonds themselves.

The engines, cars, buildings etc. were variously disposed of by Machine Tool. The Schader Company of San Francisco handled the actual removal of the track and ties under contract. The huge Barrett bridge, a dubious salvage risk, was left to stand like some silent anachronism until 1968; at that time it, too, was dismantled in conjunction with the raising of Exchequer Dam to create a larger reservoir on the river. The Merced Station was used as a Teen Kanteen for a few years and was finally sold to a local contractor who moved it three blocks away. It is now used partly as an office building and partly as a German restaurant. The Merced Freight Station collapsed under the rigors of moving and was dismantled. Most visible signs of the railroad disappeared from Merced in a short time, and the populace turned to other things.

LEFT: *Largest fan trip over the YV, May 30, 1945, sponsored by the Northern California Railroad Club and the Los Angeles Railroad Boosters.* ABOVE: *A. D. Schader Co. workmen dismantling YV in 1946.* (*Leon Bartholomew*)

Although its life span was short by many standards, the YV had its share of exciting events. In October, 1909, President William Howard Taft and a party including Governor Gillett, Senator Flint and three congressmen made the round trip to and from the valley on the YV after a great ceremony in Merced.

In the 1920's a considerable number of Hollywood favorites including Doug Fairbanks Sr., Mary Pickford, Mae West, Buster Keaton and Fatty Arbuckle to name a few, had their autos and themselves transported from Merced to El Portal and return via the YVRR. Special loading platforms were built at each terminal to load the early day autos onto flat cars for the overland trip to and from the valley before the building of the all-year highway.

The YV was even in the movies. In 1922, famous cowboy star Tom Mix shot scenes for a silent film epic, *Trouble Shooter*, near Bagby using railroad facilities.

Prince Gustaf Adolphus of Sweden, and King Albert, Queen Elizabeth and Prince Leopold of Belgium were among the foreign dignitaries who sampled the sights of the Merced canyon on the YV.

Perhaps the most famous train was President Roosevelt's special in August, 1938, when engines 26, 29 and 25 led a festooned delegation into El Portal and back again. In the halcyon days of private railroad cars, the YV hauled many a millionaire to the valley in regal fashion on the back end of its regular run.

Delegates, conventioneers and special groups of all kinds often chartered their own trains for the Yosemite trip. In 1939 alone, there were 79 special passenger trains over the line.

Arrival at Park of Pres. Taft and Party Merced, Oct 6 1909

President Roosevelt's Special in August, 1938. LEFT: Brakeman Henry Loggins beside bedecked No. 29. ABOVE: Festooned train shed at El Portal awaiting Roosevelt arrival. BELOW LEFT: B & O observation with loading ramp and speaker's rostrum at El Portal shed. BELOW RIGHT: View of ramp used by President who was unable to descend steps at that time. (Henry Loggins collection)

The YV had its share of wrecks. Mostly they were minor in size and involved only a single train or a mis-directed car. Several employees and passengers lost their lives in individual accidents down through the years, how-ever. What was probably the worst wreck in YV his-tory didn't kill anyone at all although Engineer Al Yoakum was seriously injured. Yoakum, piloting engine number 28 and carrying a delegation of New Jersey doctors and nurses to a Yosemite convention on July 7, 1920, suffered fractured ribs and lacerations when spreading rails derailed his train and plunged the engine and several cars into the canyon. The locomotive was almost totally wrecked and several cars were badly smashed. Yoakum credited the saving of his life to the fact that medical aid was imme-diately available in the persons of the surgeons in the passenger list who ministered to him at once. Number 28 was eventually repaired but bore a large dent in the side of the tender which was visible in every later photograph.

There is still much of the YV in evidence for the railfan and tourist even today, if one knows where to look.

The National Park Service is constructing a railroad museum at El Portal, and caboose number 15 is on display along with a three-truck Shay that had absolutely nothing to do with the YV but is similar to the engines formerly

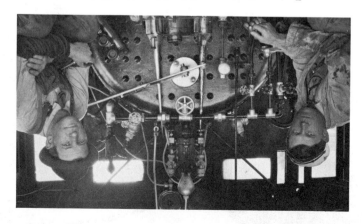

Engineer Yoakum on left with unidentified man.

LAST-MINUTE NEW

ENGINEER INJURED IN DERAILMENT

MERCED, July 7.—Al Yoakum, the engineer, suffered a broken rib and was otherwise injured when the locomo-tive and baggage of a Yosemite valley train, bearing a num-ber of the New Jersey delegation to the democratic con-vention, was derailed yesterday at a point two miles above Dagby in the Merced river canyon. A special train brought the passengers and injured engineer to this city.

employed in the woods by the Sugar Pine Lumber Company.

The caboose, of 1890 vintage, was purchased from the Colorado Midland by the YV in 1922 and saw service until the line was liquidated. A Santa Barbara railfan, Leon Bartholomew, bought it for $250 in 1946 when the equipment was being disposed of by the Machine Tool Company. Bartholomew paid a fare of 17c a mile to have it towed by a Southern Pacific freight from Merced to Los Angeles and back up to Santa Barbara over the Tehachapi Loop, a distance of 378 miles. It was in such rundown shape at that time that the SP towed it behind its own caboose at the extreme end of the train for fear of breaking it in half.

After 13 years of serene existence as a railroad club headquarters, the caboose was sold by Bartholomew to the Park Service and it was trucked to its present resting place at El Portal in 1959.

The old roadbed of the YV is plainly visible all along the Merced canyon and a number of trestles and bridges still stand, with some being used for auto traffic by residents of the area. When Bagby was flooded in 1968 as a result of the raising of Exchequer Dam, the Bagby station and turntable were moved to El Portal by the Park Service and now form an integral part of the transportation museum.

42

Caboose No. 15 as it looked after arrival in Santa Barbara in 1946. It was pulled by a steam locomotive for the last time at Santa Barbara when it was moved to the end of an industrial siding, loaded on a low-boy truck, and hauled to a vacant lot for use by the Channel Railroad Club. (Leon Bartholomew)

Scars of the two famous inclines mark their locations below El Portal and there is even an old box car or two rotting quietly here and there in the canyon. At Merced, a dozen or so former employees will fondly recall the old events when asked, and there are plenty of tourists still returning to the valley who took the never-to-be-forgotten ride to Yosemite in their younger days.

But mostly, the cars zip along the all-year highway with little thought by the hurrying sightseers of the turning, twisting line that used to lie just across the river.

Tourists continue to pour into the valley in ever-increasing numbers and few take the time to learn about the railroad that helped so much to develop the whole area long ago.

But once in a while, on a late summer afternoon, if you stand at just the right bend in the river, you may hear the faint sound of a train whistle echoing up the canyon, and you'll remember (or imagine) how it used to be 30 years ago when old 21 came puffing around the turn and headed for El Portal with a load of excited tourists out to see the wonders and the glories of the Yosemite.

Those were great days in the valley and they deserve a place, along with the railroad, in its history.

The YV is gone, but surely not forgotten.

May her memory stay ever green in the hearts of those who loved her.

TIME TABLE

a. m.	a m	p m	mi			am	a m	p.m
	3 15	2 40	0	Lv .... Merced .... Ar		11.00	12.15	2.30
.....		3 02	17	.... Edendale		10 37	...	1.30
	3 55	5 19	18	..... Snelling		10.22		1.40
8.30	4 08	3 34	24	.Merced Falls............		10 09	11 23	1200
9 32	.....	4 07	37	....Pleasant Valley........		9.32		11 25
9 58		4.20	41	.... Mast........		9.19	.....	11.25
10.20	5.15	4 40	49	.... Bagby........		9.00	10.10	10.07
a. m	6 50	6.20	79	.... El Portal .... Lv.		7 25	8 30	11.45
	a. m	p m		Ar.		am	p m	

O. W. LEHMER
Supt. and Traffic Manager
MERCED, CALIFORNIA

C. H. WRIGHT
Local Agent

43

ABOVE: *A 1909 YV timetable. The 79 mile trip between Merced and El Portal took about 3½ hours. It was virtually the same for the next 35 years.* BELOW: *No. 20 at Snelling Station in 1910. (Frank Robinson)*

LOCOMOTIVES

This sampling of YV motive power shows the remarkable similarity of equipment. The YV owned 9 steam locomotives in its lifetime and 7 were still in action when the line was broken up.

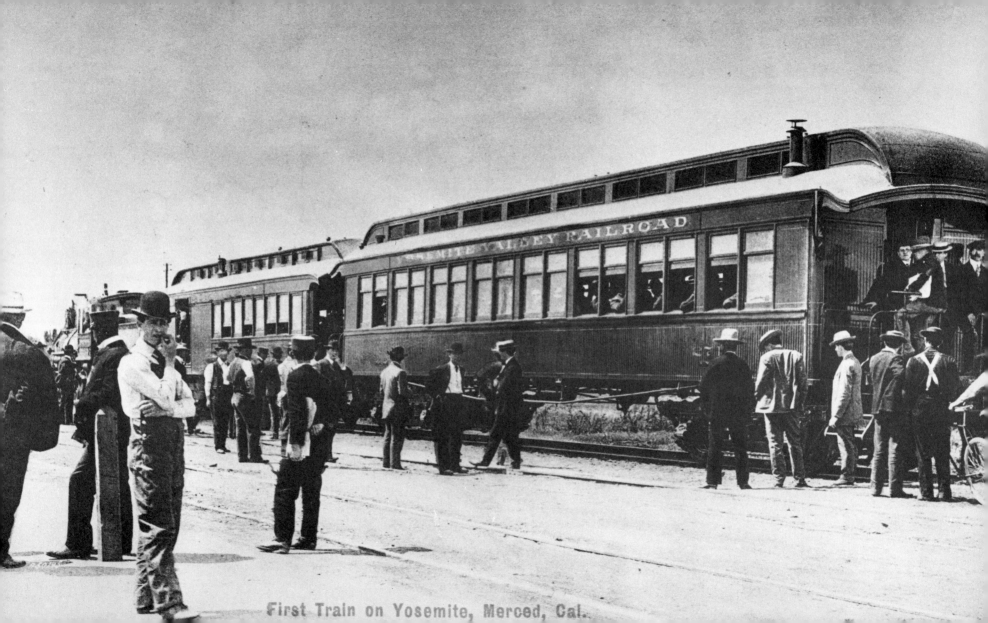

First Train on Yosemite, Merced, Cal.

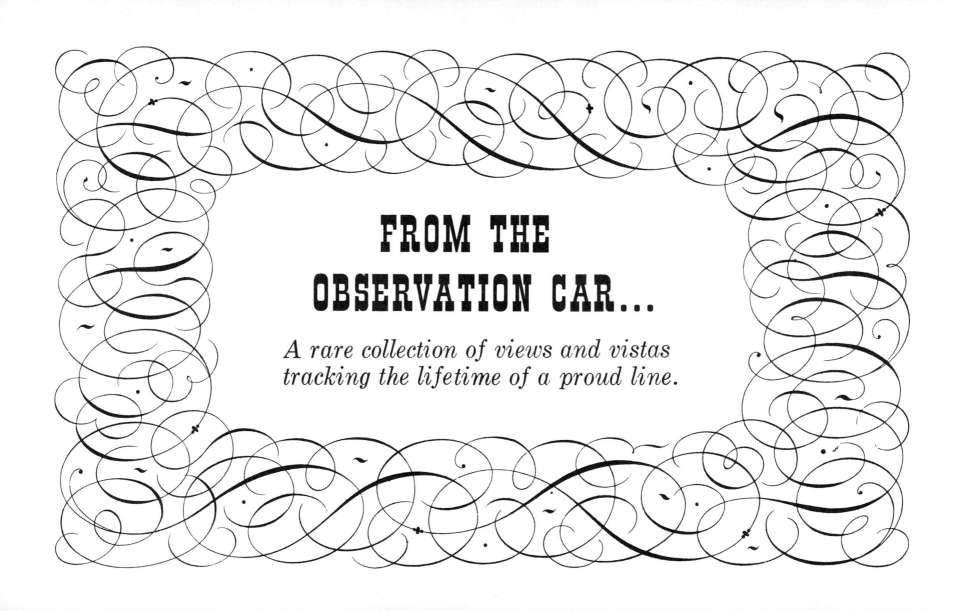

FROM THE
OBSERVATION CAR...

A rare collection of views and vistas
tracking the lifetime of a proud line.

48

Stage coach on the road built by the YV between El Portal and the valley in 1908. The trip took an hour and a half by horse-drawn open stage. This road is now used as a portion of the Arch Rock entrance to Yosemite National Park. (Author's collection)

Rustic El Portal depot shortly after completion in 1907. (*Author's collection*)

Mixed train crossing the Bagby bridge. (*Fred Stoes*)

Hotel Del Portal in 1908. Early YV travel folder advertised the hotel as "modern and first-class in all respects with hot and cold water, electric lights, steam heat and large veranda." The 4 story hotel was operated by *W. M. Sell* and had 100 rooms, 30 with bath. It cost a reputed $50,000 to build, and after it burned to the ground in 1919, it was replaced with a smaller hotel farther down the hill.

51

ABOVE: *YV log train heading for the Merced Falls mill. The route from Incline to the mill was downhill nearly all the way so light motive power could be used.* (*Fred Stoes*) RIGHT: *Second incline of the Yosemite Lumber Company built in 1923. Not as steep as the original incline, but nevertheless an imposing sight.* (*Kramer Adams collection*) FAR RIGHT: *Rare photo looking down the spectacular first incline across from El Portal. The dips and rises on the 8300 foot operation are apparent in this 1912 picture.* (*Clara Boyd collection*)

54

LEFT: *Donkey steam engine of the Yosemite Valley Lumber Company hoisting itself to the top of the first incline in 1912. This was a counterbalanced incline designed so that a loaded car descended as an empty one ascended. There was a single track from the base to a point about midway of the incline where a passing switch was situated. The lowering engine was geared to a 12 to 1 ratio and provided a car speed of 600 feet per minute. The time required to lower a car varied from 10 to 12 minutes including the time necessary to attach the cable at the summit and detach it at the foot. The 6 x 19 plow steel cable used was 1½ inches in diameter. (Clara Boyd collection) RIGHT: Extra No. 26 log train at Incline in 1942. Man in cab is Ken Monson, with Jakie Williams in gangway. (Bob Lunoe)*

OPPOSITE AND LEFT: *Two more photos of construction of first incline in 1912. A number of trestles were built across gullies with a large trestle at the base across the Merced River. Note double trackage of passing area in second photo. (Clara Boyd collection)*

57

OPPOSITE PAGE: *Log train wreck caused by broken axle near Bagby in 1932. (William St. Jeor)* LEFT: *Loaded log car No. 884 descending second incline. Five foot high steel bulkhead at front end of car prevented logs from sliding forward.*

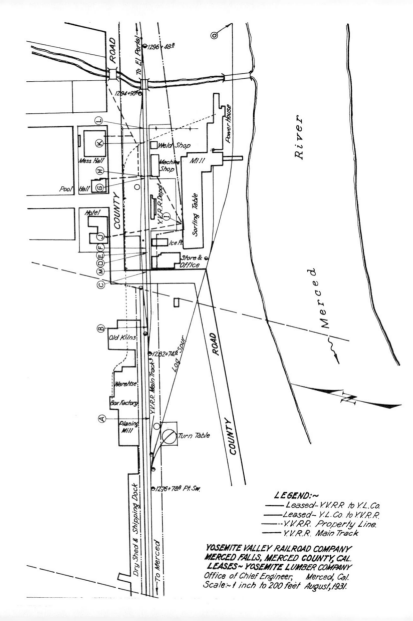

YOSEMITE VALLEY RAILROAD COMPANY
MERCED FALLS, MERCED COUNTY, CAL.
LEASES ~ YOSEMITE LUMBER COMPANY
Office of Chief Engineer,   Merced, Cal.
Scale:~ 1 inch to 200 feet   August, 1931.

ABOVE: *Chief Engineer Grant Nickerson on 1927 inspection trip with Thomas Colvin, a visitor.* (William St. Jeor) LEFT: *Layout at Merced Falls from 1931 YV files.*

A very early YV train at Merced station. Officials at rear of train include General Manager W. L. White at left, Superintendent Frank L. Higgins second from left, and Chief Engineer Grant Nickerson in center. (Clara Boyd Collection)

EASTBOUND TRAINS HAVE RIGHT OVER WESTBOUND TRAINS OF THE SAME CLASS.

YOSEMITE VALLEY RAILROAD COMPANY

EASTWARD — TIME TABLE — WESTWARD

No. 71 — September 3rd, 1929 — STATIONS

No. 10 Freight (Leave Daily Except Sunday)	No. 8 Freight (Leave Daily Except Sunday)	No. 2 Passenger (Leave Daily)	Miles from Merced	Ruling Grade Ascending	STATIONS	Ruling Grade Ascending	Miles from El Portal	Capacity of Sidings	Fuel, Water, Turn Tables, Wyes and Phone	No. 3 Passenger (Arrive Daily)	No. 9 Freight (Arrive Daily Except Sunday)	No. 11 Freight (Arrive Daily Except Monday)
		5:55 AM	0.0		MERCED—S. P. Depot.		77.7	5		5:15 PM		
		6:00	0.5	0	MERCED—Y. V. Depot.	0	77.2	YARD	WFTYP			
				0	MERCED—S. Fe Depot. (0.5)	0						
			1.0	15	A. T. & S. F. Crossing (3.4)	15	76.7					
			4.4	20	Bellevue (6.5)	35	73.3					
		f 6:18	10.9	40	Edendale (4.3)	37	66.8	1174		f 4:53		
		f 6:27	15.2	23	Hopeton	0	62.5	620		f 4:45		
		s 6:33	18.1	23	Snelling (6.1)	0	59.6	913		s 4:40		
7:20 PM	9:00 AM	a 6:50	24.2	41	MERCED FALLS (2.4)	0	53.5	YARD	F.W.T.P.	4:28	5:00 PM	2:55 AM
7:28	9:08	6:58	26.6	53	Morse (3.0)	0	51.1	401		4:20	4:46	2:44
7:38	9:18	7:09	29.6	53	Star	0	48.1	1343		4:10	4:33	2:31
7:42	9:22	f 7:13	30.7	53	Exchequer (3.0)	0	47.0		P.	f 4:07	4:28	2:26
7:52	9:32	7:24	33.7	53	Ellis (3.4)	26	44.0	482		3:58	4:15	2:13
7:59	9:39	f 7:31	35.7	0	Barrett	21	42.0	1381	P.	f 3:52	4:07	2:05
8:13	9:53	f 7:45	39.1	0	Jasper (1.8)	10	38.6	294	W.	f 3:40	3:51	1:49
8:19	9:59	f 7:51	40.9	0	Detwiler (3.3)	0	36.8	1402	P.	f 3:34	3:44	1:42
8:30	10:10	f 7:59	44.2	53	Kittridge (3.5)	0	33.5	438	P.	3:25	3:10	1:29
8:50	10:27	s 8:12	47.7	53	BAGBY	0	30.0	1378	W.T.P.	s 3:15	2:55	1:15
9:10	10:47	f 8:28	53.5	53	Lehmer	0	24.2	481		f 2:57	2:25	12:40
9:17	10:54	f 8:34	55.5	53	Kocher (0.6)	0	22.2	348	P.	f 2:51	2:16	12:31
9:19	10:56	8:36	56.1	12	Harte (1.7)	0	21.6	1480	P.	2:49	2:13	12:28
9:35	11:12	f 8:49	60.8	53	Briceburg (2.4)	0	16.9	485	P.	f 2:35	1:54	12:09 AM
9:43	11:20	8:55	63.2	42	Drum	0	14.5	1622		2:28	1:44	11:59 PM
9:57	11:34	f 9:10	67.0	53	Emory (2.8)	0	10.7	840	W.P.	f 2:16	1:27	11:42
10:10	11:47	9:20	70.4	53	Bloss (1.2)	0	7.3			2:06	1:12	11:27
10:14 AM	11:51 AM	f 9:24	71.6	62	Clearinghouse (1.4)	0	6.1	80		f 2:02	1:07	11:22
10:27	12:07 PM	s 9:30	73.0	79	Incline (2.0)	0	4.7	YARD	P.	s 1:58	1:00	11:15
10:35 PM	12:15 PM	9:35	75.0	79	Moss Canyon (2.7)	0	2.7	2200	W.Y.	1:53	12:20 PM	10:40 PM
		9:55 AM	77.7	105	EL PORTAL (77.7)	0	0.0	YARD	T.P.	1:45 PM		

Footer — Eastward: Arrive Daily Except Sunday | Arrive Daily Except Sunday | Arrive Daily. Westward: Leave Daily | Leave Daily Except Sunday | Leave Daily Except Sunday.

YV timetable of September 3, 1929.

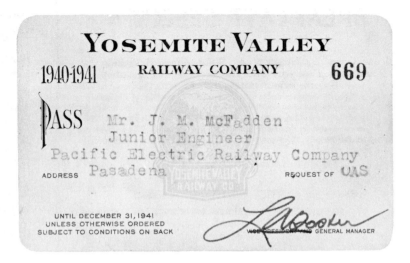

Last pass ever issued by the YV. It was given to railfan J. M. McFadden and dated July 16, 1945.

INCLINE CALIF
Fr Yosemite N P & I

Yosemite Valley Railway Company

BREAKFAST SELECT
A TABLE D'HOTE SERVICE

Please Order by Number and Write on Meal Ticket,
Each Item Desired. Waiters Are Not Permitted
to Take Verbal Orders.

FRUITS AND JUICES

Orange Juice   Grapefruit Juice   Tomato Juice
   Half Grapefruit   Prunes   Cantaloupe

No. 1—   90c Per Person
Choice of Any One Fruit Listed Above
Dry Cereal with Cream
Ham or Bacon with Eggs
Toast, Fried Potatoes
Tea, Coffee or Milk

No. 2—   75c Per Person
Choice of Any One Fruit Listed Above
Dry Cereal with Cream
Two Eggs Any Style
Hot Cakes or Toast
Tea, Coffee, Cocoa or Milk

No. 3—   65c Per Person
Choice of Any One Fruit Listed Above
Hot Cakes with Bacon
Pure Maple Syrup
Tea, Coffee or Milk

No. 4—   50c Per Person
Choice of Any One Fruit Listed Above
Dry Cereal with Cream
Toast
Tea, Coffee or Milk

Marmalade or Jam 10c

ABOVE: *No. 23 with metal baggage-postal and coach eastbound in Merced canyon in the '30s. (Fred Stoes)* LEFT: *Diner borrowed from the SP in summer months served complete meals as part of YV attempts to fight bus competition.*

ABOVE: *First passenger train over the newly completed Barrett Bridge on April 18, 1926. (Frank Robinson)*
OPPOSITE: *California Camera Club excursion at El Portal about 1914.*

Twisted wreckage from Al Yoakum wreck of 1920. No. 28 was nearly demolished and several cars were badly damaged.

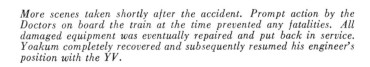

More scenes taken shortly after the accident. Prompt action by the Doctors on board the train at the time prevented any fatalities. All damaged equipment was eventually repaired and put back in service. Yoakum completely recovered and subsequently resumed his engineer's position with the YV.

Y.V. Special to Merced-Exchequer Dam Dedication June 23, 1926. Bent Bros, Los Angeles, Ctrs 170

68

69

LEFT: *YV special to Exchequer Dam dedication on June 23, 1926. The dam was the largest project of its kind in America at the time. (Author's collection)* ABOVE: *Front view of the Exchequer Dam and powerhouse in 1945. (Leon Bartholomew)*

No. 28 pulling a mixed train through the pastoral San Joaquin valley. The dent in the tender caused by the Al Yoakum wreck is visible in this picture. Jaunty spark arrestors were a YV trademark but probably failed to do a great deal of actual good. (Fred Stoes)

View of Merced yard and station in 1944. (Harvey Rowe)

ROUND HOUSE, MERCED, CAL.

OPPOSITE: *First roundhouse at Merced. This building burned in 1914 and was replaced by metal structure.* LEFT: *Second big incline built by the Yosemite Lumber Company. This was on the north side of the Merced Canyon and operated until 1942.* ABOVE: *Auto stages taking over for horse stages at Hotel Del Portal in 1914. The big railroad hotel burned to the ground in 1919.*

OPPOSITE: *Scrapping operations at Merced in 1947.*
ABOVE AND RIGHT: *Assorted sampling of YV passenger equipment.*

LEFT: *YLCO Shay with log train at top of second incline. Note metal engine house at left.* ABOVE: *YV passenger train in Merced Canyon about 1939. (Bill Pennington)*

ABOVE: *No. 28 and short mixed train near Merced in 1941. (Fred Stoes)* OPPOSITE: *View of El Portal yards.*

ABOVE: *Franklin D. Roosevelt's bedecked motive power at El Portal in 1938. (Henry Loggins Collection)*
OPPOSITE: *No. 28 takes water at Bagby in 1942. (Bob Lunoe)*

ABOVE: *No. 26 at Bagby's twin water tanks (Bob Lunoe)*
OPPOSITE: *Charlie Grant in gangway of No. 22 about 1911.*

LEFT: *Fine old photo of No. 29 and log train at Merced Falls mill.*
ABOVE: *Picturesque YV Box Car 609.* RIGHT: *YV Caboose No. 15 being trucked by NPS to the transportation museum at El Portal.*

LEFT: *Yosemite Portland Cement incline at Emory. A narrow gauge, internal-combustion powered railroad ran about a mile back from the top of the incline to the quarry. An average of 25 cars of lime rock per day were loaded here for YV freight during peak years. (Larry Grabert)*
ABOVE: *El Portal station during a rain storm in 1945. It burned to the ground in 1949.*

YOSEMITE VALLEY RAILWAY

IN LIQUIDATION

MERCED, CALIFORNIA　　　**TELEPHONE 28-29**

FOR SALE

The Yosemite Valley Railway has come to the end of the line. Offered for sale in part or whole, this 78 mile short-run railroad consists of small but modern and well maintained equipment.

For Further Details, Write or Wire.

All Items Are Offered Subject to Prior Sale.

LOCOMOTIVES

2—AMERICAN TYPE 4-4-0 SATURATED

Rated Tractive Power	18720 Lbs.
Cylinder Diameter and Stroke	18"x26"
Diameter of Drivers	63"
Weight of Drivers	72600 Lbs.
Weight on Front Truck	42000 Lbs.
Total Weight of Engine	114600 Lbs.
Driving Wheel Base	8' 09" (Rigid)
Total Engine Wheel Base	23'
Steam Pressure	165 Lbs.
Fuel	Oil
Valve Gear—Stevenson	

Tank Capacity
Oil	2220 Gals.
Water	4200 Gals.
Condition—I. C. C. Operating Condition	

Builder—American Locomotive Company
Builders No. 43167 and 44389

2—MOGUL TYPE 2-6-0 SATURATED

Rated Tractive Power	28600 Lbs.
Cylinder Diameter and Stroke	19"x28"
Diameter of Drivers	57"
Weight on Drivers	120000 Lbs.
Weight on Pony Truck	23000 Lbs.
Total Weight of Engine	143000 Lbs.
Driving Wheel Base	14' 02"
Total Wheel Base of Engine	22' 09"
Steam Pressure	190 Lbs.
Fuel	Oil
Valve Gear—Stevenson	

Tank Capacity
Oil	2200 Gals.
Water	4500 Gals.
Condition—I. C. C. Operating Condition	

Builder—Baldwin Locomotive Works,
Builders No. 39634
Builder—Baldwin Locomotive Works,
Builders No. 45130

3—MOGUL TYPE 2-6-0 SUPERHEATER

Rated Tractive Power	28600 Lbs.
Cylinder Diameter and Stroke	19"x28"
Diameter of Drivers	57"
Weight on Drivers	120000 Lbs.
Weight on Pony Truck	23000 Lbs.
Total Weight of Engine	143000 Lbs.
Driving Wheel Base	14' 02"
Total Wheel Base of Engine	22' 09"
Steam Pressure	190 Lbs.
Fuel	Oil
Valve Gear—Walschaert	

Tank Capacity
Oil	2200 Gals.
Water	4500 Gals.
Condition—I. C. C. Operating Condition	

Builder—Baldwin Locomotive Works,
Builders No. 58685 Built 1925
Builder—Baldwin Locomotive Works,
Builders No. 55275 Built 1922
Builder—American Locomotive Company
Builders No. 65433 Built 1924

LOCOMOTIVE CRANE

American Hoist and Derrick 18-Ton Locomotive Steam Crane, Combination Shovel and Pile Driver, Boom 27', Shovel Capacity 1 Yard.

PASSENGER CARS

1—PASSENGER OBSERVATION CAR

Construction	Wood
Seating Capacity	30

Inside Length Including Observation
End	64' 05"
Inside Width	8' 08"
Height at Eaves	11' 06"
Width at Eaves	9' 11"
Center to Center of Trucks	46' 02"
Wheel Base	8' 01"
Trucks	Steel, 4 Wheels
Axles	5"x9"
Vestibule Platform	Built Up Type
Lights	Electric, Train Line
Heat	Steam
Brakes—P-2 Valve	14"x12" Cyl.

1—VESTIBULE PASSENGER COACH

Construction	Wood
Seating Capacity	68
Inside Length	59' 02"
Inside Width	8' 10"
Height at Eaves	11' 03"
Width at Eaves	9' 11"
Center to Center of Trucks	45' 10"
Wheel Base	8' 01"
Trucks—Built Up Construction Wood and Steel	
Axles	5"x9"
Platform	Built Up Type
Lights	Electric, Train Line
Heat	Steam and Baker Heater
Brakes—P-2 Valve	14"x12" Cyl.

1—VESTIBULE PASSENGER COACH

Construction	Wood
Seating Capacity	60
Inside Length	52' 07"
Inside Width	8' 10"
Height at Eaves	11' 07"
Width at Eaves	10' 02"
Center to Center of Trucks	38' 07"
Wheel Base	8' 01"
Trucks—Built Up Construction Wood and Steel	
Axles	5"x9"
Platform	Built Up Type
Lights	Electric, Train Line
Heat	Steam
Brakes—P-2 Valve	14"x12" Cyl.

1—40-FOOT STEEL BAGGAGE AND POSTAL CAR

Builder	Pullman
Date Built	1911

PASSENGER CARS
(Continued)

Underframe	Steel
Center Sills	2 10" I Beams
Side Sills	2 6"x3½"x1/2 Angles
Couplers	Sharon
Draft Gear	Westinghouse
Body Bolster	Cast Steel
Platform	Steel
Brakes—New York	12" Cyl.
Lighting System	Electirc, Train Line
Trucks	Cast Steel
Journals	5"x9"
Length Inside	40'
Length Over Platforms Coupled	42' 11-1/8"
Baggage Apartment	24' 10-15/16"
Wheel Base	32' 1"
Weight—Total	80,700 Lbs.

1—COMBINATION PASSENGER AND BAGGAGE COACH

Underframe	Wood Construction
Seating Capacity	28
Inside Length	52' 08"
Inside Width	8' 11"
Height at Eaves	11' 05"
Width at Eaves	10' 02"
Length Baggage Compartment	28'
Length Overall	61' 10"
Trucks—Built Up Construction Wood and Steel	
Journals	5"x9"
Vestibule	Built Up
Lights	Electric, Train Line
Brakes—P-2	14"x12" Cyl.

CARS

3—30-TON STOCK CARS

Capacity	60,000 Lbs.
Cubical Capacity	1838 Cu. Ft.
Light Weight	32,900 Lbs.
Gauge	4' 8-1/2"
Length Outside	36' 1"
Extreme Height	14' 1-1/2"
Extreme Width	9' 6"
Length Inside	35' 5"
Width Inside	8' 8-1/2"
Height Inside	7' 0"
Axles	4-1/4"x8"
Brakes—New York F-1 Valve	8"x12" Cyl.

2—50-TON FLAT CARS

Capacity	100,000 Lbs.
Light Weight	34,500 Lbs.
Underframe	Steel
Length Over End Sill	42'
Width Over Side	9' 01"
Height to Deck	3' 10½"
Height Over Brake Staff	6' 03"
Gauge	4' 8½"

CARS
(Continued)

Axles	5½"x10"
Brakes	K2 Valve 10"x12" Cyl.

2—50-TON FLAT CARS

Capacity	100,000 Lbs.
Light Weight	34,500 Lbs.
Underframe	Steel
Length Over End Sill	42'
Width Over Side	9' 01"
Height to Deck	3' 10"
Height Over Brake Staff	6' 03"
Gauge	4' 8½"
Axles	5½"x10"
Brakes	K2 Valve 10"x12" Cyl.

7—25-TON FLAT CARS

Capacity	50,000 Lbs.
Light Weight	Approx. 21,000 Lbs.
Length Over End Sill	35' 6"
Width Over Side	9' 4"
Height to Deck	4' 3"
Height Over Brakestaff	6' 8"
Axles	4-1/4"x8"
Gauge	4' 8-1/2"
Brakes—New York F-1 Valve	8"x12" Cyl.

3—25-TON FLAT CARS

Capacity	50,000 Lbs.
Light Weight	22,000 Lbs.
Length Over End Sill	36' 0"
Width Over Side	9' 4"
Height to Deck	4' 0"
Height Over Brakestaff	6' 7"
Axles	4-1/4"x8"
Gauge	4' 8-1/2"
Brakes—New York F-1 Valve	8"x12" Cyl.

2—25-TON FLAT CARS

Capacity	50,000 Lbs.
Light Weight	22,000 Lbs.
Length Over End Sill	36' 0"
Width Over Side	8' 6-1/2"
Height to Deck	4' 4"
Height Over Brakestaff	6' 10"
Axles	4-1/4"x8"
Gauge	4' 8-1/2"
Brakes—New York F-1 Valve	8"x12" Cyl.

44—40-TON STEEL TWIN HOPPER CENTER DUMP STEEL GONDOLAS

Capacity	80,000 Lbs.
Cubical Capacity	660 Cu. Ft.
Light Weight	Approx. 32,000 Lbs.
Gauge	4' 8-1/2"
Length Outside	23' 10½"
Width Outside	8' 1-1/2"
Extreme Height	10' 1-5/8"
Length Inside	20' 6¼"
Height Inside	5' 11-¾"
Axles	5"x9"
Air Brakes—H-1 Valve	8"x12" Cyl.

LEFT: Quiet summer afternoon at El Portal yard in the early '40s. (Leon Bartholomew)
ABOVE: Liquidation folder published by Machine Tool & Equipment in 1946 when YV equipment was being sold.

No. 25 with a heavy passenger consist eastbound to El Portal. (Fred Stoes)

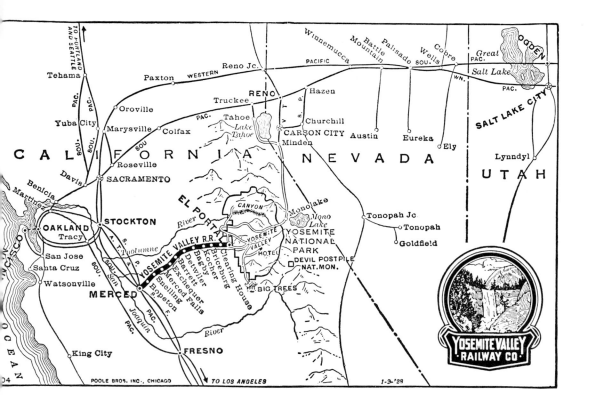

ABOVE: *Mixed train with No. 28 (note tender dent) crossing the Barrett Bridge at high water.* (Fred Stoes)
OPPOSITE: *A beautiful study by Charles Clegg as YV mixed train heads through the level San Joaquin valley on a summer day in 1944.*

View of original incline across from El Portal taken in 1962. The growth of 40 years of underbrush has failed to cover the right-of-way and local residents have strung a TV antenna up the mountainside opening.

This very situation may perhaps portray better than any words the changes that a half century has brought to the American way of life. Progress is sometimes more than a little painful.

END OF TRACK

"It has come at last, old friend, it has come at last—
The time when you and I must say goodbye..."

LOCOMOTIVE ROSTER

LOCOMOTIVE NUMBER	ORIGINAL COST	BOILER NUMBER	BUILDER	DATE BUILT	TYPE	BOILER PRESSURE	DATA	DISPOSITION
20	No Record	C-254	No Record	No Record	4-4-0	No Record	No Record	Sold to F. L. Fletcher 1925
21	6,248.40	A-21	From Wabash R. R.	1881	4-4-0	148	63 - 17 x 24 - 94,000	Sold to A. E. Perlman 9/45 Scrapped 1946
22	13,589.42	43167	American Locomotive	1907	4-4-0	165	63 - 18 x 26 - 114,600	Sold to A. E. Perlman 9/45 Scrapped 1948
23	14,734.99	44389	American Locomotive	1907	4-4-0	165	63 - 18 x 26 - 114,600	Sold to A. E. Perlman 9/45 Sold to Modesto-Empire Traction 7/47 Scrapped 8/47
25	27,999.36	58685	Baldwin Locomotive	1925	2-6-0	200	57 - 19 x 28 - 143,000	Sold to A. E. Perlman 9/45 Scrapped 1948
26	30,883.76	65433	American Locomotive	1924	2-6-0	200	57 - 19 x 28 - 143,000	Sold to A. E. Perlman 9/45 Scrapped 1948
27	17,340.18	39634	Baldwin Locomotive	1913	2-6-0	200	57 - 19 x 28 - 143,000	Sold to A. E. Perlman 9/45 Scrapped 1948
28	19,851.18	45130	Baldwin Locomotive	1917	2-6-0	200	57 - 19 x 28 - 143,000	Sold to A. E. Perlman 9/45 Scrapped 1948
29	27,541.77	55275	Baldwin Locomotive	1922	2-6-0	200	57 - 19 x 28 - 143,000	Sold to A. E. Perlman 9/45 Sold to Mexican Railroad 1948

BACK COVER: *A fine YV action photo by Lucius Beebe, America's foremost railroad chronicler.*